Rocks on a Platter

WESLEYAN POETRY

Barbara Guest

Rocks on a Platter

Notes on Literature

Wesleyan University Press

Published by
University Press of New England
Hanover and London

Wesleyan University Press

Published by University Press of New England, Hanover, NH 03755

© 1999 by Barbara Guest

All rights reserved

Printed in the United States of America

5 4 3 2 1

CIP data appear at the end of the book

Contents

I.   "Ideas. As they find themselves . . ."   1

II.   *"And the words linger, deciding which direction to take . . ."*   13

III.   "Intimacy of tone . . ."   21

IV.   "Without shyness or formality . . ."   35

I

To live is to defend a form . . .

HÖLDERLIN

all about contradictions

to find yourself - such a strange modern notion
how do you prepare to
inhabit a particular time period

Ideas. As they find themselves. In trees?
To choose a century they are prepared to inhabit. Dreams set by
typography. A companionship with crewlessness - - shivering fleece - -

interesting connection

Ship

shoal   rocks

to approach this land raving!

Rocks, platter, words, words . . .

mammoth teeth.

Mobility interseamed with print: "a small car beside the porch and wind
with a harsh caress . . ."   another STORY BEGINS:

A DONKEY DRAWS A CART TO THE FURNACE AND
THE CHILDREN PRESS AROUND, THEIR SMALL TEETH
GLOWING.

I heard the wolf.

looming doom

3

It had been a vagabond voyage and the entrepreneur was fatigued, yet held up his head inflamed with "LITERATURE, the ABSURD." Ideas dropped off vines and into his mouth. An idea fell off a SECULAR vine roaming his head: BAKED APPLES!

Among his listeners, a waterer of his vines, was a beautiful girl who hand-typed A BOOK CALLED "BAKED APPLES." THESE ARE STORIES THAT "MELT IN THE MOUTH," said the critics.

THE KING   READ *BAKED APPLES 100,*
AND GAVE HER AN APPLE TREE GROVE.
THE KITCHEN MAIDS, who had written JONQUIL TALES, asked the king for a jonquil grove. "I prefer BAKED APPLES," said the King.

TEARFUL, THE KITCHEN MAIDS CLOSED THEIR KITCHEN AND OPENED A JONQUIL STORE IN BUDAPEST, WITH YELLOW DOORS, and GREEN CEILINGS THAT VERY SOON APPEARED IN A FILM "THE BRIGHTENING OF BUDAPEST."

(The King, who liked the film, donated 25 white Palace chairs.)

Passivity . . .

pollen indoctrinated AND fragrance.

She digs with her fingernails into the earth while speaking and

weeping. Her face is also

introduced into the story:

a fragrant narration.

"ASTOUNDING BEING ALIVE!"

Pockets jingle   highly responsive place in the shelter
        of those rocks   at last the jingle of your pockets

HEARD ON THE PAGE.

. . . in its contiguous
treatment of time, literature.

is inclined to divorce
the uninhibited   aroma of BEAUTY, OR
SPECTACULAR LEAP

suspicious
of fragmentation,

or *sweet reproach of invisibility.*

7

Tradition

Tantamount to theory

    treacles
         of tender truckland

    near Trebizond.

TRIUMPHS.

    A TREMENDOUS TUNE-UP.   ORTHODOXY.
tremendous   tune-up

    tra- la-la.

Wet earth disinters itself.

With aplomb

    bestows

        "The Kiss behind the Counter."

Implacable poet.

Shattered rocks

                              hid in the rock?
Deft, vehement.   Amulet cast from the pocket.

And wind over red-tiled roof   and we grow closer
to the moss of subjectivity   guarding an iron basin
        limed,   old stars.

                Rays   modern rays,
                          modernly, so be it.

Noise of the shattering!

            Behooved us to welcome tonality,

        or succumb to the theme of inharmony . . .

            "where we once were."

Fiction and Complice

torment the mineral kingdom,

feathering the page
in the merit of feather.

Of brokenness - -

brokenness   resembles
            evasion (although not separate), and
with a coat of arms,

' afloat with the telling.'

II

To invest abstract ideas with form,
and animate them with activity has always
been the right of poetry . . .
DR. SAMUEL JOHNSON

And the words linger, deciding which direction to take.

Will they remain with the middle chord? The atonal section is

fearful, running along beside the pale brook, clouding and declouding.

Aching

time interrupted   discontinuous treatment.   After the piping
          MURMUR unlocked   inclined to advance toward the desire
                    to hasten an ending or

          avoid the spectacular jump - -;

drifting into invisiblity,
                    as does remnant of self.
          A blow is merciless - -;

          solid objects are merciless.

          OLD SHOE.

Hullabaloo, Hullabaloo

Again, are you more *tactile in* handling

the body

pressed against you?

Is the pear-shaped manuscript

endangered?

Alas, its honied drip.

The honied drip.

The empirical sun

       on the disturbed border
in the animal-clad wood   gone down,
magick within   begs extension
disappointed   at eye level:
grey-streaked sky, sea.

                 Less
          less mourning less
             sandy mourning!

Frail sentence moved by

the seismic sway of existence

under a shaken tree

is cultivated outside us.

Words, inflammable,

        lie   in bricks

          this changes.

                         White
perpendicular lights   attached to the shoulder
I touched the wrist with my writing finger   and from the center
the orb of the eye was enough fire   to light the writing lamp and
afterwards   the blade   withdrew from the writing shoulder   and
that writ
blew away   flame lit with nothing   and nothingness stayed.

          Skin of the lost paper
                Knuckle smooth   (touched the writing).

                Nietzschean   thumb on
                      the trout
                and they disappear.

III

. . . the empirical inner and outer world
is just what is not the world of genuine reality,
but is to be entitled a mere appearance more strictly
than is true of art, and a crueller deception.
HEGEL, *Introductory Lectures on Aesthetics*

Intimacy of tone

and form

beyond the tangible itinerary

mirror trap

at 30 degrees

I have the impression of a long body;

of loaves and fishes,

of "belles lettres."

Wisdom in travel several palaces

        latitude without margin --

        silver-toned blow up --;

arm in a sling and hawk chin

   you are also a hawk --

you walk in hawk shadow a guise --.

Sad rose, Rilke charm

        lodged in a castle --

bone button sewed to a coat --;

snow footprints adieu

cold tears splashed acre is intimacy,

        and many chimed things,

        future's conduit.

. . . to recapture   early days   cats-cradle.

    Mont Blanc   Childe Harold

demons. a tooth bends down on the 'd'.

   Transubstantiation   only a web

  is permanent dent   on the body and ablaze.

               Shoulder ablaze.

In a room

    "not alone"

enters

    midday

    appears

massive.

In the faded game you won the top with the green scratch you win,
I alter the text "did not win the top" put "earned" white flag.

Four in the entertainment room, you and someone with a foreign name,
I forget.

He has written out a plan and glued it to the text. He told me

he is a king himself entering life on a whim,

language attached, gerunds.

In the loneliest hours to share a flamboyance,

an attraction to distance and disappearance.

Beyond the roof tiles,
lap of a hill, *fleur d'or,*
gold ass on the threshold
Apuleius' other.

Cannot dream except in "two's" or be alone, is hollowed out.

Of many colors   porcelain

               with faerie glove

you betray   (biography).

dissident morning!

with no ulterior purpose

image exchanged for a feather

le poisson on watered page.

Apparition shape of thy head

finds its verve,

        ivy the poem

shoving it into the stain,

        weight in the room,

        I promise.

Here the dream began, two voices, one joking, this took place in sleep, you remember, and the other caressing, a tussle between the joking and the caress, points of view caressingly and jokingly; they often sighed between joking and caressing, the hiccup, an odd note the hiccup, between the joking and caressing; perhaps a lapse in the dream.

PHANTOM

       (reverie)
         (passion)

       in canoe

of twelve-tones

       or *Helen in Egypt*

Bar of silence crossed the mouth

decorates it.

       She watched skirts sweep the floor,
       from that day of her sixteenth year
       her skirt brushes the floor. What she is after

       "trailing skirt," blossom
       in mimetic hair

       fills some other Body.

IV

The Moment a limit is posited
it is overstepped, and that
against which the limit was
established is absorbed.
ADORNO, *Aesthetic Theory*

Without shyness or formality:

"a gesture of *allowing oneself time*"

Remember how starry it arrives the hope of another idiom, beheld
that blush of inexactitude, and the furor, it
will return to you, flotsam blocked out.

compose, like Schoenberg, *poem* music

"robustly"

"flotsam of the world of appearances"
drifting by and out of the picture,

where the throne disappears . . .

now in robust position,
NAMING,

naming the throne, *"flotsam of appearance,"*

ALLOWING TIME.

Is evanescence the wool beggar?
strike that simpleton

"Bafflement."

Thee GLOSS GLOSS

point to the Mix, and

there! it slides into view
the Dolphin,

before the moment oversteps,

into

the *hum* pour his ivory.

And is this what they mean by *transfuse?*
  the hum pouring into another,

              the furnace turned down,

         snowy apricot furnace
  of the dolphin.

  And the rage disappears,
intellectual rage over grandeur.

         Swimming off in the twilight
         is the Dolphin, what occurs
         absorbed in the skin.

Grandeur oversteps,
artificial and strange, lifting

a leg above *glitter* . . .

The rule of thumb under *glitter*
is that *glitter* disturbs, and

paled, finds painting

a wild grape loosens

glitter
from the *rock platter.*

Ovid writes,

"Earth, painted with flowers, that *shone brightly,*"

Pictaque dissimili flore nitebat humus.

How does the pickled axe maintain itself . . .

is the desire of the stone figure
                    to outlive a sheepfold?

Bittersweet and decisive the urn
            when showed a technique
        of maintenance in the dark field and modernly.

That pickled axe

is the anima, entry into waterfield,

            is the wax waterfield,

                    and savaging.

. . . pumpkin glazed in the sun
no alphabet, no grief.

Overstepping the farmstead to make way
in the underbrush for a faun-like portrait,

                    sweet pumpkin.

The sight of the arm
  even in the cornfield there it is found
with three racing women   hair grown
over the forearm   was considered upside down
and rumor of a complicated series of burials
lent a deshabillé   not usual on ancient ground
no one could have foretold   uncovered according
to various ideas
about sacred places.

And ingenuity   follows the silvered
     montage into a new elevation

As if whispered.

An episode with new palm trees.

Words in magnetic order

Words in natural order.

Vulnerable Dolphin skin

and magnetic skin.

In the new part about palm trees

stumbling to multiply

tall palms, to replace

a fanatical order (*Orlando*

Furioso or *Dolphin Empire*)

sensuous *en effet,*

and near the sea basin

rustle of the palm trees

introduce   (and a similar movement among their
leaves)   then the Dolphin slow.

Where are they, *wood nymphs and the glittering*

Beings -- do they overstep each other . . . ?

The Dolphin God -- does he swim on the page?

* * * * * *

"*In ancient times*
Heavenly Beings made sense of themselves and how
they have made off with the strength of the Gods."

Hölderlin

University Press of New England publishes books under its own imprint and is the publisher for Brandeis University Press, Dartmouth College, Middlebury College Press, University of New Hampshire, Tufts University, and Wesleyan University Press.

About the Author

Barbara Guest has published fourteen volumes of poetry since 1960, as well as a novel entitled *Seeking Air* (Sun & Moon, 1996), the biography *Herself Defined: The Poet H.D. and Her World* (Doubleday, 1984), and *The Confetti Trees: Motion Picture Stories* (Sun & Moon, 1999). She has earned many awards, including the Longview Award, the Lawrence Lipton Award for Literature, the Columbia Book Award, an NEA fellowship, and the Poetry Society of America's Frost Medal.

Library of Congress Cataloging-in-Publication Data
Guest, Barbara.
Rocks on a platter : notes on literature / Barbara Guest.
   p.   cm. — (Wesleyan poetry)
ISBN 0–8195–6372–2 (alk. paper). — ISBN 0–8195–6373–0 (pbk. : alk. paper)
I. Title. II. Series.
PS3513.U44R64   1999
811'.54—dc21   99–23471